Mother Tiger
and her cubs

Story by Beverley Randell
Illustrations by Julian Bruère

Mother Tiger
had three little cubs
to look after.
She hid her cubs
in a hole in the rocks.

She stayed in the hiding place, too.

One day, Mother Tiger said,
"I am very hungry.
I have had no food for a week.
I will have to find a pig to eat."

"My cubs are asleep," she said.
"Now I can go down to the river."

Mother Tiger
went down to the river,
to look for a pig.
She hid in the long grass.

"I am so hungry," she said.

The little cubs woke up.

They went outside the hole

in the rocks

to look for Mother Tiger.

They cried out for her,

but she did not come.

She was down by the river.

9

The sun went down,
and a pig came to the river.

Mother Tiger jumped out
of the long grass,
and she got the pig.

Mother Tiger
ran all the way back
to the rocks.

She went inside the hole,
but her cubs had **gone**!

Mother Tiger ran outside.

She cried out to her cubs.

The cubs cried out, too,
and then they ran over to her,
one by one.

Mother Tiger fed her cubs with milk.
And they all went to sleep
in the hole in the rocks.